ALSO BY ALEX DIMITROV

POETRY
Love and Other Poems
Together and by Ourselves
Begging for It
American Boys

NONFICTION
Astro Poets: Your Guides to the Zodiac
(with Dorothea Lasky)

ECSTASY

ALFRED A. KNOPF • NEW YORK • 2025

ECSTASY

Poems

Alex Dimitrov

Published by Alfred A. Knopf, a division of Penguin Random House LLC, 1745 Broadway, New York, NY 10019.

Knopf, Borzoi Books, and the colophon are registered trademarks of Penguin Random House LLC.

Portions of this work originally appeared in the following publications: *The Atlantic:* "Today I Love Being Alive" and "Tuesday"; *The New Yorker:* "Everything Always," "Monday," "Someone in Paris, France Is Thinking of You," and "The Years"; and *Poetry:* "Birthday in Palm Springs."

Library of Congress Cataloging-in-Publication Data
Names: Dimitrov, Alex, author.
Title: Ecstasy : poems / Alex Dimitrov.
Description: First American edition. | New York : Alfred A. Knopf, 2025.
Identifiers: LCCN 2024020079 (print) | LCCN 2024020080 (ebook) |
ISBN 9780593802922 (hardcover) | ISBN 9781524712693 (trade paperback) |
ISBN 9780593802939 (ebook)
Subjects: LCGFT: Poetry.
Classification: LCC PS3604.I4648 E27 2025 (print) |
LCC PS3604.I4648 (ebook) | DDC 811/.6—dc23/eng/20240506
LC record available at https://lccn.loc.gov/2024020079
LC ebook record available at https://lccn.loc.gov/2024020080

penguinrandomhouse.com | aaknopf.com

Printed in Canada

1 3 5 7 9 10 8 6 4 2

The authorized representative in the EU for product safety and compliance is Penguin Random House Ireland, Morrison Chambers, 32 Nassau Street, Dublin D02 YH68, Ireland, https://eu-contact.penguin.ie.

This book is for lovers & virgins everywhere.

Life is an ecstasy.

—RALPH WALDO EMERSON

CONTENTS

†

†

ECSTASY

THE YEARS

All the parties you spent
watching the room
from a balcony
where someone joined you
to smoke then returned.
And how it turns out no one
had the childhood they wanted,
and how they'd tell you this
a little drunk, a little slant
in less time than it took
to finish a cigarette
because sad things
can't be explained.
Behind the glass and inside,
all your friends buzzed.
You could feel the shape
of their voices. You could
tell from their eyes they were
in some other place. 1999
or 2008 or last June.
Of course, it's important
to go to parties. To make
life a dress or a drink
or suede shoes someone wears
in the rain. On the way home,
in the car back, the night sky
played its old tricks. The stars
arranged themselves quietly.
The person you thought of drove
under them. Away from the party,
(just like you) into the years.

ECSTASY

At the end of ecstasy
only the memory of ecstasy.
The tongue. The chorus.
The streets of flesh.
Blur of the highways.
Blue of the lakes.
Jesus's mother.
Jesus.
Our city of New York.
A pill. A dollar. A hundred.
Your father's face.
The bridges at night.
The heart outside the heart
and the VACANCY signs
with the NO right above.
How long till we get there?
How long is the night?
How fast will misery make us its keeper
when the memory of ecstasy wanes?
Like the summer that's over.
Like the green lights that pass.
Fireworks. Funerals. Weddings.
The freedom you looked for in people.
The freedom you lost when you did.
And after the lawns of childhood.
And after the graves ahead.
After whatever ecstasy is
and the feeling of knowledge.
Past pleasure. Past whatever
gets you off next.

SOUL FUCKING

The bathtubs at the Bowery Hotel
are exceptional but better alone.
Like sex in general because
fucking yourself never gets old.
Lunch is the saddest meal of the day
and October is beautiful.
It should come around twice.
But it doesn't. Some things
are singular. I think of you always
even if people tell me you're terrible.
What do they know about
soul fucking anyway?
It's sad how even sex
becomes eating an orange.
Exciting at first and then
juice. Only juice.
And I know we never fucked
but it was like standing
in front of a painting.
More interesting than
knowing the artist as friend.
We will never understand
one another in this world. Not really.
We are unknowable as each winter
or what people who jumped
from the towers thought of that day.
No one knew me exactly like you did.
A person eating an orange.
Walking up Bond Street.
Trying on shoes I'll never wear
just to see myself as somebody else.
There is no true self.

No one gets to the bottom of anything.
I only wanted the soul
and I'd soul fuck you
anywhere. Anyway.
I could watch you
peel an orange forever.
And right before death
we think of everything small.
I'm willing to bet on this.
Not sex or why evil exists.
Not where the soul lives entirely.
More like a face that has
recognized yours from a distance.
A voice making itself real
in the moment before
you actually turn.
You are that moment for me.
You are the turning.
And yes, I will soul fuck you
into eternity. I will soul
fuck you like nobody else.

TODAY I LOVE BEING ALIVE

I wake up and eat a banana.
Stand naked in my kitchen.
Shave and listen to Billie Holiday.

My god, I'm so obsessed with you.
You're new. You're tall. You make me feel
like never putting clothes on.

Who's to say if you'll still be around
when anyone's reading this poem.
Or if the Earth will continue

(it's getting very hot!)
or if we'll get it right in language
exactly how we feel about each other.

I don't care about being remembered.
I care about a great glass of wine.
Strong men. Beautiful sentences. Italian leather.

Call me old fashioned, really.
But when I cut myself shaving above the lip,
I lick up the blood. I don't wince.

SOMEONE IN PARIS, FRANCE
IS THINKING OF YOU

This poem is happening in Paris, France,
where it's raining and we're all so drunk
that it's impossible to keep a secret.
Every morning the waiters say *bonjour*
and every morning I drink my coffee
with a kind of American sadness
they've started saying *hello*.
Hello, beautiful man I'll never have
on Rue Charlot. Hello, woman smoking
by the Seine and closing her eyes
between drags. We're all lost, even in Paris,
and if this place won't take my mind off you
I guess I'm in love and in for more rain.
You are the man on Rue Charlot
somewhere in Brooklyn, peeling an orange
and thinking of buying a suit.
I would like to be an orange in that suit.
I would like all the men on Rue Charlots
across the world to put in their resignations
and stop torturing me. Let me chase fire
on another street, in another country
where someone takes out the orange
and peels it. And puts it slowly to their mouth.
There's a pause. The woman closing her eyes
opens them. The lights on the boulevards come on.
Someone smiles. Someone sighs. Someone lingers.
Someone in Paris, France is thinking of you.

SOMEONE IN NEW YORK CITY
IS THINKING OF YOU

I think one of my plants is gay
because he loves Pellegrino
and is extremely photogenic.

When I killed off all his friends
(since I was always in Miami)
I decided it was time for sparkling.

He deserved it! He hung on!
And now he watches me writing poems
from the windowsill where he is truly happy.

I wish I had you like I have my plant.
We would take baths in Pellegrino
and walk to the Met to see the Cubism show

even though we both hate Cubism.
You're not a blond but sometimes
in the afternoon light I imagine you

as Richard Gere in *American Gigolo.*
I guess he wasn't blond either.
I guess it doesn't matter what you are

as long as you're naked
and somewhere in France eating oranges.
We would be there forever.

Naked and French and all our friends
would call to say: *boys! Don't you think
you'll come home now?*

But we'll never come home.
Never call back. We just wouldn't care.
We'll drink Perrier like the locals.

MONDAY

I was just beginning
to wonder about my own life
and now I have to return to it
regardless of the weather
or how close I am to love.
Doesn't it bother you sometimes
what living is, what the day has turned into?
So many screens and meetings
and things to be late for.
Everyone truly deserves
a flute of champagne
for having made it this far!
Though it's such a disaster
to drink on a Monday.
To imagine who you would be
if you hadn't crossed the street
or married, if you hadn't
agreed to the job or the money
or how time just keeps going—
whoever agreed to that
has clearly not seen
the beginning of summer
or been to a party
or let themselves float
in the middle of a book
where for however briefly
it's possible to stay longer than
you should. Unfortunately
for me and you, we have
the rest of it to get to.
We must pretend
there's a blue painting

at the end of this poem.
And every time we look at it
we forget about ourselves.
And every time it looks at us
it forgives us for pain.

I was just about to throw on a shirt
and take the Q to Canal and walk
to Bacaro and have five glasses of wine
and then I felt guilty I haven't written
much of anything so I said, "Okay,
you have twenty minutes to write a poem,"
and here I am, eighteen minutes left,
writing a poem about writing a poem.
Okay! So I'm done being obsessed with men
who don't know I'm a genius. Bye baby.
Bye big mouth. Bye small dick. I won't even say
the last one's name because he already thinks
he's in my poems and it's the closest
he'll ever get to love. But hold on,
this is turning into a truly cruel poem.
Let's rewind! Let's have a drink.
Let's actually order the squid ink
pasta when we get to Bacaro
and take two bites then go out for a cigarette
around the corner so the guys at Clando
(who've spilled out onto the street)
can look at me and pretend they're not cruising
and pretend they're not gay, and I'll pretend
I care about the bad novels they're writing
or how "everything is political,"
someone has to say this mid-conversation,
and I have to go out for another cigarette
because I'm thinking I should go to 169 Bar
at this point but don't, I go to Fong's
with Will and David and a beautiful Scorpio
who looks like Joni Mitchell (who is
a Scorpio, obviously) and the way I see it

with thirteen minutes left I have nothing
to prove and nothing to teach you,
and this poem is not going to solve
any crisis or pretend it knows anything
about anything, and the way I imagine it is
someone puts on The Smiths at Fong's,
which has actually never happened
but this is a poem and I can do what I want
since truth has nothing to do with art
and art has everything to do with truth
and you're probably wondering
what Smiths song and why a Smiths song
and when is this poem going to be over
(two minutes now, I lost a little time
trying to gain a little speed)
and it's "William, It Was Really Nothing,"
that's the song, it's not great for the cadence
of the poem but it's the one Smiths song
I want to hear at a bar and never will
because it's too sad and too short
and too beautiful—and not everything
beautiful gets what it deserves. Okay!
Life is pain. I think we all know that.
It's fine. Whatever. Just play the next fucking song.

SUNRISE

Walking toward it on Twenty-Ninth
I unbutton my coat in the wind
and light a cigarette easily.
There's no one on the street
except for a guy in a suit and a boy
coming home from last night.
I've been that boy so many times
though I rarely wear suits.
I've stopped at the bodega he stops at,
lost keys at the bar one block down,
gone on dates I hardly remember,
because time is the oldest story
and this city doesn't give a shit about
anything old. *It's an illusion,* my friend
used to say while we danced in some
basement in the late aughts
high on coke and so much X.
It's an illusion you feel this way
so wait til tomorrow, wait til two drinks
from now, wait til you meet someone else.
And though I never listened to him
something about this sunrise
makes me remember that.
It makes me feel like, yeah
I'd trade wisdom for youth.
I would do it. Any day. I don't care.

TUESDAY

When I can't talk to anyone
I like to sit in front of water.
If I have a minute to feel good
I take that minute. I have a cigarette.
I walk into the museum of past lives
and rearrange all the chairs.
This poem is meant to be read
at the bar on a Tuesday
when you're dehydrated
and not feeling so great.
I want to know you
like a dog touches the wind
with its tongue. I want to know
why time moves impossibly slow
when pain rises, and what makes it
speed up like two people
looking for each other
at the end of the night.
When was the last time someone
looked at you like a bridge
held by cold air? Like the cars
flying down the FDR
taking us where we imagine
is better than where we are.
I imagined it differently also.
I imagined more than mixed feelings,
tough leather, the last yes coming
so quickly. Men and how they
pace awkwardly before parting.
Cats and how they roam
freely in bodegas at dawn.
The towers in photos.

The tulips of April.
The person in a theater
now watching the credits,
reading the names, stalling
to put on their coat or their scarf
or their gloves. Or maybe
not stalling. Maybe they're
waiting for the music to change.
Not everything is an ending.
Not anything's worth believing.
And you can begin anytime
like this whole world began
out of nothing. You can walk out
tonight and feel totally new.
All you need is the right pair of boots.

100%

After years of being in love
with the wrong people
I'm still open like The Paris Theater
on 58th Street. I walk up
and down Sixth Avenue
thinking of who I was six years ago.
The waiters at The Odeon
wink at me. A woman
in a gold dress drinks alone
and men in suits talk of the market
which is up like my libido.
Hello, God. What now?
Will I ever learn how to cook
and not use my oven for sweaters?
Will I stop expecting the French to love me?
Will I carry an umbrella on days
when it says 100% rain?
What is 100% rain exactly?
How could anyone be that certain?
Not even love feels that way
and again I'm the person
telling strangers more than I should.
The person nodding yes
instead of no. The person
who wouldn't return to the past
even if I had an umbrella.
Why bother? 100% it's not
as good as whatever this is.

ANOTHER PARTY

An orange streak in the sky!
Before I go in I smoke
with the roses on Fifth.
They're drenched from the rain
and perfectly dressed.
The party is beautiful.
The windows are French.
The windows are open
though it's not time
to jump out of them yet!
I would gladly
take another life
with less ice in my drink.
Which I bring to the boys room
and text people I shouldn't
because I'm a mess.
I'm emotional!
It's the truth, I think,
listening to gossip
swimming around
while I fix my hair
and decide what to do
with the rest of my time
here on Earth.
It's good to be talked about!
It's serious not to die!
And when I come out
even the blond painter
I never liked nods at me.
We're all going to the same
afterlife together.
A place that doesn't seem

to have any clocks
though it's exactly 10:37
and even you
(who are so far away
and may never be closer)
somehow cross the edge
of the room or my mind.

HELLO

Just now someone
I imagined a life with
enters the bar.
The gin arrives.
The clocks speed up.
I take off my jacket.
The night finds my face.
I am swimming
in the midnight haze
of another American summer.
Hello!
I am swimming
in the lakes of childhood.
Of course!
I am swimming
toward you and know
you'll remember
that August, the sky,
the rooms we would drink in.
The smell of your hair.
The smell of my hair.
The solitude in love.
The companionship in solitude.
But most of all everything ever
(even the fire) that's happened
to slightly lost but very forgivable
people like us.

EVERYTHING ALWAYS

A man dangles a cigarette
over a fire escape on Crosby.
It's so early, I am still in last night.
All of life honks.
The streets steam.
Gin changes to coffee
and I think of you less
then I think of you often.
How strange! To be a person
instead of a tree. I'll miss it.
I'm in it! I watch a bucket
of peonies glint in the sun.
The wind moves through the avenue.
A woman loses her hat.
I lost something back there
but what use is turning around?
Goodbye to the past!
I buy leather pants.
I call my mother.
Someone has written
everything always
over the pavement
and I nod because I get it.
Isn't it time I move to Greece?
Today I only have time
to walk to the water.
I do that. I love it.
Who wants to go home, anyway?
Who wants to be what they are?

1995

Got to America on July 3.
Kurt was dead. Someone
called me a virgin who can't drive.
The boys wore Vans and pretended
to be skaters. The girls pastel
sweaters and plaid skirts
I never looked at but thought
I could rock. Later. Yeah later.
See you. As if. Whatever. I was
a murdered angel for Halloween.
Blond Chris was a football player.
Travis was Jesus. The night
Blond Chris choked me I thought
I would die. I said, yeah.
That's good. Keep going.
Just fucking end me.
Travis's mom wanted to fuck
Bill Clinton. She quizzed us
on the Presidents (capital P)
and every time we forgot
she'd say, Okay. Now again
and from the beginning.
In order! Alright. Jesus.
I had all of Hole's
Live Through This
in my head.
I didn't have room
for the presidents, sorry.
Though you know,
I never forgot JFK.
Must be the face.
Must be a Catholic.

Must have been November
when Blond Chris
asked me the only
real question anyone's
asked me on Earth.
The number one song
in America was "Fantasy."
I threw up my lunch
every day around 12:33.
What do you want to be,
he said after school by the track.
I don't know, I said.
What do you want to be?
Blond Chris wanted
to be a football player.
I wanted to start a band.
Like Nirvana, he said.
No, like Jesus, I told him.
The years passed.
We still talked.
I grew out my hair.
Blond Chris got a girlfriend.
The fantasy ended.
He broke his arm
and had to sit out the season.
I found Rimbaud
and decided it was
better than bands.
Because in a band
you still have to
talk to people.
Because I already knew
how to do this.
I knew what poetry was.
I was always alone.

BLOND SUMMER

If pornography was set to more emotional music
so you can almost pretend they're in love.
If sometimes you need someone a little more ugly
and sometimes you need someone as ugly as you.

Blond Chris in the summer of 1999.

In the grass. In the grass where you're kicked
in the mouth and you take it.
In the grass where you don't cry
and swallow the blood (you're a boy).

Blond Chris in the summer of 1999.

You're a boy and you steal the white tulips.
You're a boy. You put the tulips in your mouth.
The tulips are yours now. You want to ruin the tulips.
They are in your mouth. You're a boy.

Blond Chris in the summer of 1999.

If you watch them spit. If you smile.
If they catch you watching.
If they spit on you. If you like it.
If they never smile and have beautiful knives (they are boys).

Blond Chris in the summer of 1999.

Blue life. Blue pain. Blue slap.
Little shake. Don't drip.
Don't cry. Don't talk. Just smile.
Blue day. Blue God. Blue something.

Blond Chris in the summer of 1999.

Why would you step on the bodies to watch all the insides spill out?
The beautiful bees and the beautiful wasps.
Listen to me like you would a school teacher.
Someone is going to nail your hands to the wood for a very long time.

Blond Chris in the summer of 1999.

Honey. Baby. Good boy.
Don't touch. No touching.
Open your eyes. Open your mouth.
Open your throat like a man and learn to keep it open.

Blond Chris in the summer of 1999.

I was going to write you the most delicate letter
but when I came home I couldn't tell what I was.
Oh God. Oh Jesus. Oh Mary.
What the fuck am I supposed to do with myself?

Blond Chris in the summer of 1999.

You were my God once
but you know I have always been stronger.
And you were my blood here on Earth
but all you did was piss on my fear.

Blond Chris in the summer of 1999.

If you're a good boy all you get is nothing.
Too good. Too sad. Too handsome.
Better not to have been anything then.
Better then to have been something ugly. Someone bad.

Blond Chris in the summer of 1999.

I miss you in the long afternoons.
I miss you under the trees.
I miss you in the long afternoons under the trees.
And I miss you under the trees where I was a person in summer.

I was.

IN DEFENSE OF OBSESSION

I walk blocks in the wind
thinking of you like a lion.
And imagine your hand in my mouth.

POPPERS

B says he doesn't
believe in true love.
I say shut up
and get us a drink
before I kill you.
Inhale. Okay.
What do you want, he asks.
True love, I tell him
(and inhale again
this time longer
so I feel super fucked).
B thinks it's insane
I'm a romantic
but it's also why
he hangs out with me
all the time. He's bi.
We're at 169 Bar
in the bathroom
and there's no mirror
and I hate it
but the night feels good.
We've been in
bathrooms like this
a million times.
We know how to move
around each other
and navigate
shit spaces because
this is New York.
And November.
And nothing
like I imagined at all.

When B leaves
the bathroom
I stand there
a little light headed
thinking of what to do
with the rest of my life.
The job of a poet
is to chase a feeling.
The job of a poet today
has become kissing ass.
And I never liked ass.
I'm more of a dick guy,
actually. More of
a faggot and clearly
a poet and real poets
(Emily Dickinson
once said) don't kiss ass.
That's the thing, I tell B
when I stand next to him
at the bar a minute later.
People who are cynical
are just afraid of being happy.
Are you happy, he asks me.
I'm not, I tell him.
But I'm willing to chase it
the same way I'm willing
to chase dick or poetry
(forever and like
nothing could stop me
not even kissing ass).
So shut up then, he says.
And go chase it.
We kiss. I pull on his belt.
The bartender looks at us
in a sort of hot way.

Yeah okay, I say,
and take the bottle
from his fist.
We go outside
where everything
good is and I tell him
the outside has always
been better than the inside
for fags. Happiness
isn't within. Poetry
is not a self-help book.
Fuck the self. And fuck help.
None of these married people
are happy. Yeah, B says.
Fuck it all. And let's
get fucked somehow.
For sure, I nod.
And give him back the bottle.
He opens Grindr.
Someone across the street
throws up. It's the Aries
new moon and I'm
going to change
my entire life.
Who's gonna stop me.
But before that
we smoke a cigarette
and I stare at B's jaw
and we go in to drink.

XANAX

There was little to remember
and the past was a lake I swam through
in a white dress which I never took off.
The way skin is a layer thrown over
the animal soup of the body.
The way Christ bled out.
The way a stranger's cock fills you.
The way it feels to blow money
on some dead afternoon in December
when the world is as gone as you are.
You know, God, I said.
I wish you would nail me
to something I won't return from.

On Rue de Bretagne I stood
and I was a blond.
I was alone that summer
and many people and things
passed through my mouth.
Who are you? My therapist
asked every Wednesday.
I'm not sure, Jonathan.
I need a glass of rosé.
A chain around my neck.
To be hit even when I've been
good (and especially good).
Who are you? I loved him
for saying it that way.
He wanted to know more than I did.
I put so many vodka soaked olives
in me at Little Red Door.
I told Luka I loved him.
I told strangers more
of my life than I did my own family.
How everything was falling apart
the way it does at the end of love.
Which is a different grief
than death, my friend said
but it's lonely and not a street
you want to live on for long.
Whatever. I waved her off.
I stood on Rue de Saintonge
and a man on Grindr offered
500 euros to fuck me.
I was surprised. 2000, I said.
I bought cherries from Monoprix

and ate them on the street.
They were bad. And I knew
that they would be. There was
a fruit market two blocks down
but everything I wanted
that summer was bad.
I wanted to feel empty.
I wanted to be even worse than I was.
1000, he said five minutes later.
And I said okay. I'll take a bad deal.
Just be cruel, I told him.
And he double tapped on my reply
to assure that he would be.
Who are you? I'm not really
anyone, Jonathan. I'm not
really here. That's who I was
for 1000. For 2 I would have
put on a show the way Jesus did
when they killed him.
And Jesus was everywhere with me
those days in July. I wore him
around my neck. I drank holy water
from the church on Rue du Temple.
I couldn't remember names
and I couldn't remember hours
especially after ten, after sunset
after everything I thought I wanted
was here and not mine anymore.
I wasn't solar powered.
I wasn't electric.
I kept reading Alex Dimitrov
over and over in tweets
from people I'd never met.
Trump was convicted.
Carlos Alcaraz won the French.

The boys at Charlot became
the boys at Bacaro
and they knew my face
and they knew my order.
A bottle of Chablis.
A bottle of Côtes du Rhône.
So many texts sent from that bathroom.
The bar. Some place inside me
that knew I was asking
for something no one could give.
I walked Rue des Archives every night
with Lana's "Flipside" on repeat.
The last minute and forty seconds
when it's just the guitars.
I became those guitars.
I became no one's friend.
No one's son.
No one's lover.
At La Perle I fell asleep
in a booth. Jerked off
someone's friend wearing Carhartts.
Found Maxime and Emile
and two beautiful Russians.
The war continued.
My rage continued.
I stacked so many
le gramme bracelets
on my wrists I thought
I was made of metal.
The screensaver on my phone
was a 16th-century German armor
breastplate with the crucifixion
etched over the heart.
And the heart too continued.
What choice did it have.

Somewhere on a terrace
overlooking the city
the Eiffel Tower blinked
through the night.
I passed out in my boots
and my chains and my armor.
Every morning at 5
I'd wake up and take off
my clothes. Take a xan.
Try to sleep again like a real person.
What's a real person, Jonathan?
What's being a person at all
this far late in the night.
I smoked only Sobranies.
Returned no more texts.
Sent every call to voicemail.
Blew money mindlessly each afternoon.
Not because I had it.
But because I wanted to dig
so far down, if I left myself there
how could anything touch me.
You know, Judas was obsessed
with Jesus. Their kiss. His face.
Everything about him
and how the criminals were him.
The prostitutes. Sinners.
The poor. The wretched.
And Jesus, the first one of us maybe
to find out that anyone who wants you
will surely betray you.
Anyone who wants you (turns out)
may not love you at all.

KNIFE TATTOO

I stayed too long and said too many things.
Not one cab on Columbus.
Crossed the park and went home.
It was late. Handsome men
and their dogs roamed the lawns.
I could smell them.
See the shape of their shoulders.
The outlines of their cocks in their pants.
How could you look at me like someone
who's never had his tongue
down your mouth? At the party,
I don't think they should have
given me a steak knife.
Or sat us across from each other.
I'm not a pacifist. I don't like sugar or milk.
I smoke cigarettes only with people
who have them. Or men who know
how to cook difficult meats.
The blood pooled on my plate.
I ate nothing and drank the last of the wine.
Are you sorry, you said in the hallway.
Where I was a person searching for my coat.
The windows were open.
Manhattan was cold.
One of our friends looked at us
and knew exactly what we were.
It was terrible. Isn't it terrible
to be people no one can fix.

HEART TATTOO

What else then? Haven't I kissed
enough men in Brooklyn apartments.
Ran my tongue on the rim
to taste more of the salt.
Asked for the last cigarette.
Not texted. Jerked off
someone's boyfriend. Not liked it.
Left the party without telling anyone.
Moved to Miami without telling anyone.
Vials of K with a blond in Divinity School.
Lines of blow with a blond who took crypto.
A stranger. An ex. Someone I wanted
to sleep with but never did.
Someone I slept with too many times.
What else then, you said.
Don't you think you're a little impossible.
Don't you think you're avoidant, mercurial,
petulant. Just a bit of a dick.
I nodded. I put on my sunglasses.
I left a big tip then I left because baby.
Baby. Baby. Baby.
What part of life has felt possible to you?

PINK TESLA

Three boys. White shirts.
Black jeans. Pink Tesla.
If I wanted summer
I could smell the sweat
on the back of their necks.
Crush a pill and slip it in gin.
Be blessed by a body
on Collins with tattoos
of Jesus and Mary
up to the beard.
O god what did I want
that winter. I mistook
everyone with a mouth
for a heart. Took off
my clothes but kept
my socks on. Shared blow
with strangers who did more
than play with my hair.
It could have been June
but it was really December.
I could have been golden
but I was just baby dumb.
You know, one of them said,
I love it when you act like
a dumb bitch who knows nothing.
I love it when you do nothing too.
And nothing but what you are told.
So that's who I was every day.
I was solar-powered baby.
I was electric.
Good for the environment.

Good for the taking.
Just an all-around
very good American bitch.

BLUE PORSCHE

Over here it's always summer.
Men dry their bodies by the pool.
A boat passes. An American flag
floats across the horizon.
Someone talks about buying a gun
and I stare at my phone
reading texts from men
who have little to say.
I'm not sure what love is
but I know it's not this.
I don't need another drink
but past noon my body
burns in the heat. One day
it will burn off completely.
One day this place will flood
and no one will save us.
No matter how righteous we've been.
No matter whose dick is up
for the next great American jerk off.
I'm just a little brain dead, you know.
Hungover under an umbrella,
I'm parched. Starved.
Obviously glistening.
Pleading the fifth because I'm guilty
of everything. Saying *okay thanks*
when a man in a blue Porsche
takes me home.

GOLD AMEX

The city glitters like a gold Amex.
A guy lifts his shirt and shows you his scar.
You lose your ID. The palms rustle.
Someone asks if it's Tuesday
and a blond fixes his brow
before dipping a dollar
in the last of the blow.
He fingers your gums.
The guy with the scar leaves.
It's midnight. Somewhere
American jocks do deadlifts
and play video games.
Pupils shot. Mouths slack.
Chugging from their cups
with such devotion they spill.
On their perfect stomachs.
A whole circle of them.
Groping their shorts and yawning.
That room everyone hates
and wants to stay in forever.
Watching them win.
Watching them kill.
Passing out with clothes on again.
(Beginning of summer.)
Pretending you're smarter.
Pretending you've grown up somehow.

WHITE AUDI

And that summer I forgot about pain
when there was pain. And that August
I wore white, drank red.
The blow dotted my stache.
And when they continued
asking him to see if he hadn't od'd,
if his mind was still there, if his lips
were just accident blue and not
dead blue. *He lifted himself up*
and some of us thought it was a joke.
Others took photos and story'd.
I gave him my sunglasses.
Someone covered him in a shirt.
And he said to them . . .
(though no one knew who he was,
and everyone wanted to fuck him)
he who is without sin among you
(but you know, that was a different party;
not in The Grove, not in the year 2020).
And I can still see his face
and the way he looked at me
when he came to.
When he pressed his hand
against a palm for balance.
And we called him a car.
A white Audi. I never knew his name.
Or if he got home. Or why
he didn't have clothes on.
But baby if you've ever been lost
and if you've ever been sad

and done something you shouldn't.
You nod. And you linger. You make do.
You don't *cast the first stone.*

BLACK MERCEDES

Somewhere in Monti
I was lost like Monica Vitti.
Smiled so the Italians loved me.
Wore my crucifix under my linen.
God was very far away.
1.2 miles exactly.
I unbuttoned my shirt
and walked through the piazzas.
Licked the sweat off my lip.
Licked my fingers
after eating a pastry.
God was in a black Mercedes.
In an Adidas tracksuit.
That's all he told me.
Asked if I was boyish
so I sent him a photo.
Down Via Cavour
I looked at every black car
and tugged at my dick.
The boys glistened.
I took a piss by someone's Vespa.
I want to find you
I typed it out in Google translate.
Voglio trovarti. Then nothing.
God went silent.
My shirt was drenched.
The city was burning.
Someone's father smoked
a cigarette and read the newspaper.
Baby. Won't you tell me the news.

JESUS

In the video the boy
is asked to strip down
to his socks and chastity cage
although he's doing it
willingly before he is told.
His eyes are hazel.
He's lanky. Wiry.
Still quite tall even as
he kneels and looks up
at the men who have lined up
to piss in his mouth.
He doesn't flinch or tire.
His Adam's apple moves
up and down faster than
swallowing anything
I've wanted badly before.
And when a tear rolls down
his cheek toward the end
(from the job itself)
it goes all the way
to his pecs and settles,
where his name is tattooed across.

BABY

The last days I was a virgin
I got a speeding ticket.
Split my lip at a party.
Lost my wallet.
Stole a shirt from Sean's bedroom.
Put it over my face.
Read my palm.
Read Rimbaud during math class.
And I was blond with black roots.
And I was thorns over roses.
Every night in a parking lot somewhere
I said dear God
let me cum
with only people I love.

BABY, NO

Oh fuck what I wanted.
The morning was green
then the morning was blue.
The skyscrapers glittered.
I opened a window.
Chrysanthemums came.

And all through the fog, you said.
And into what else, I thought.
How the lake filled with honey.
How the dark knew itself.
And the strong pill ran through me.
And the day was mere chance.

Baby, baby, baby.
A few drinks, a few maybes.
A little of this and a little of that.
So when God came to a party on Bowery
I stared at my phone and I hid in the hallway.
I really thought God would be somebody else.

KETAMINE

I want to go back to that summer
and be in a k-hole with you forever.
Me + You carved on a tree with a knife.

HIGHWAY

I went to Switzerland that winter.
The lake was full of birds.

The women carried flowers.
And God forgot the world.

I know, I know
that even the highest branches

(even the highest branches will be touched).

And men are maps of evening.
And weather's all we have.

And only the sky
whenever I'm with you

(whenever I'm with you)

is a highway I've been on before
is a night lost in June.

WEDNESDAY

They've planted the loudest
yellow tulips on Fifth. A cab
almost hits me as I stand there
looking at them. I am possessed!
I'm not dead. People are out
on the steps of the Met
though it's closed.
A man playing saxophone.
Two boys in Supreme.
A Dalmatian. A Bulldog.
They look even more
taken care of than me!
Yeah well, I'm not surprised
(I'm kind of a brute).
Now a guy with a stereo on his bike
plays "Juicy" and the traffic
picks up. Yes, it's Wednesday.
Yes, we're in the middle of life.
Or at least the week! It's too easy
to be sad. Everything is a lie
but everything is still beautiful.
These strangers showing up
for their meetings and dates.
Dog walks and errands.
I've forgotten Van Gogh's
Self-Portrait with a Straw Hat
is right here but that's not why I came.
I don't really have a reason.
I just love this running around
even if I'm not free.

THURSDAY

I'm only just a little lost,
I tell my bodega guy at noon
as I down another coffee
and listen to Chet Baker
who once had all his teeth
knocked out during a fight.
What I love is how that
makes him sound like a boxer
even though he wasn't,
even though I'm not really
a poet—I'm a boxer truly—
and who has ever thought
about the feelings of boxers
except other boxers who know
heart is really all you have.
I'm so tough I could live this life twice
smoking and drinking through it,
wearing pearls with flannel,
yawning at the opera,
standing by a jukebox
never asking any man
to take me home. Yeah,
that's right it's six o'clock
and I see the Empire State Building
rising in the distance. Lighting up.
A classic in the evening.
Accompanying me to dinner
where I will sit alone and order
a vodka martini from the bartender
who is the new bodega guy,
who is my new lost father,
and every boxer needs a father

and every father needs a boxer
because fight is really all that counts.
Some nights when it's close to two or three
I think: come on, you have to be a person.
You have to get home. Do something
normal. Do one thing just like everybody else.
But that's the thing about New York.
No one teaches you anything.
Or everyone teaches you something.
I'm not really sure. I'm just gonna do it my way.
I'm gonna ignore the news and the fads
and the outrage because baby—
heart is mostly all I have.
That and some fight on the side.

FRIDAY

I'm too bored to fuck
I tell my hookup so he leaves
and here I am, alone again,
inside the morning and my bed
where I text the west coast
things they won't read for hours
because they're always in the past.
Wake up! It's Friday. There's a war.
And also a great sale on denim.
But now that skinny jeans are out
my mood has fallen like the markets.
I have nothing to wear and nothing
to live for. Once more I'm here
writing this so I won't get drunk
at 4pm. "No, never!" I say to the doctor
when he asks me if I'm sad.
Depressed. Despondent. "No!" I tell him.
"And plus your new haircut
really makes you look like Keanu."
He blinks. He doesn't get it.
I'm mortified. I leave. I get a drink.
It's 4:52. What did I do all afternoon?
In another life I'll have self-control
or actually be happy.
Has anyone ever had both?
Has bombing other countries
ever worked? I don't think so.
I'm anti war and anti feeling
sorry for yourself in poems.
Maybe my doctor just didn't like
The Matrix. Maybe I should adopt
a dog so I don't have to get a boyfriend.

Maybe (even though skinny jeans
are over), when they bury me—
and I do hope it's on a Friday
so people can get their shit together
on the weekend—maybe, just maybe
I'll be allowed to dress however
I want. And eat whatever I like.
And drink whenever I please.
And my hair will look perfect forever
because that's what death is, right?
That's where we're all going
and that's why we're all drinking
and fighting and acting so vicious.
What's wrong with us, really?
What are we doing here?
I'm convinced we all just need to get laid.

SATURDAY

I thought life
would go on forever
like Saturdays when we were young.

SUNDAY

The streets before sunrise.
The first memory. The daybreak.
That place where runners
make paths into spring
and the park is eternally true.
The glint of the buildings.
The fog of our past lives.
The first yes. The last no.
The cabs flooding highways
with people again.
The clear sky. The Hudson.
The gold light of Sunday.
All this time I thought I knew.
All this time I thought we would change.

SUNSET

I remember watching it with you
and staring only at your face.

GLUTTONY

It was the winter I flew
to Miami every week.
Slipped off my shorts.
Slept in the sun.
So easy, everyone kissed me.
So dumb, I tried not to think.
Locker 89. It was mine.
I met a couple in front of it once.
Hydrated only with champagne.
Ate almost nothing.
Saw no one but strangers
and palms; I was blessed.
And when one of them asked
to come to my room so I could
piss in his mouth, I said yeah.
I said sure. I said why not.
I drank so much champagne
it turned to water.
Wine to blood.
Bread to flesh.
My piss was so pure,
it was clear. It was hot.
It was there to cure everything.
And whenever I'd stop
he'd say, *don't.*
He'd say, *drink more.*
He'd say, *just don't stop drinking.*
Because once you've had what you want
you just want it again.

LUST

John smoked cigarettes in the parking lot.
Brett cut himself by the bleachers.
Blond Chris pissed on the welcome sign
and Trevor did too. He took out his dick
easily. He didn't need an occasion.
Brett and Brian were brothers.
They sat next to each other in Bio.
Legs touching. Eyes blank.
The beginning of summer.
End of the school year.
Doors and windows wide open.
What are you doing after Bio?
I don't know. What are you?
John had a girlfriend he hated.
Brett punched a wall.
He got caught with a joint
and was suspended.
Michael left his boxers
in the lockers. They disappeared.
Brian said he would murder my face
and John drove me home.
We lived next door to each other.
Trevor said, *You're not even real.*
You're not a real boy.
Blond Chris laughed and I agreed.
I smoked and was mostly
like all of them. John. Brett.
Blond Chris. Trevor. Kevin.
The radio playing from
someone's car. Headlights on.
Stolen beer from John's dad.
Brett's knife. Michael's boxers

after he found out I had them.
And I had to promise I'd never
do it again. And I had to say it
over and over while begging.
None of us really that scared.
All of us sort of still hard.

SLOTH

All I did that summer was jerk off and smoke.
There was nothing left of my American youth
that could fill me back up.

The men who punish me first
are the ones I most understand.
Like learning about divine chastisement
in childhood. Why I had to sit alone
for an hour after putting my hands
in another boy's mouth.
How I'm good at being ignored.
I can take it. And once
let a nosebleed run
so everyone could look.
Used a knife on a suit
(not mine) and left multiple
stabs in the wool. Sometimes
it's good to destroy things.
Animals know this. The first dog
I had was named Richie
and they put him down
for biting a man on the street.
As if he should have known
everything can't be a piece of meat.
As if you can believe those
who perform righteousness in public.
On the internet in front of others.
On the street when no one looks.
Have you ever turned away
from someone who needed help?
Without reason or guilt.
Without care or concern.
Do you blow money in the middle of the day?
Do you think about cheating?
Would you do it if no one found out?
What if you had to decide who to save:

someone you fucked once
or someone you loved and can't stand?
If you had to die alone (as punishment)
for the cruel things you've done,
which ones would you repeat?
Who would you feel justified in hating?
What wouldn't you hide?
How much would you take without giving?
If you knew you had one day to live,
what evil could you finally admit to yourself?

If I used language such as
first-generation queer immigrant experience.
If I jerked off over communism and read Marx
in a Brooklyn apartment paid for by my parents.
If I hadn't been born under communism.
If I didn't know what living under communism meant.
If I hadn't been queer. Immigrant. First-generation.
If I liked enough righteous tweets on the internet.
If I wrote enough righteous tweets on the internet.
If I used the word *politics* more often.
Like in a poem written in 2011
titled "This Is Not A Personal Poem"
where I'm *so political* (but not in the right way).
All humor and irony must be excised
in an effort to further clarify intent.
As in a legal document or a piece of legislation.
If I didn't have an imagination.
If I didn't feel sorry for myself.
If I didn't feel sorry for myself on the internet.
If I wasn't cordial or diplomatic because I'm a poet.
If the job of the poet is now to be cordial and diplomatic.
If I respect my family enough not to sell their stories.
If I respect Bulgarians enough not to speak for anyone.
Gay pride sponsored by Chase bank starts now.
And I bank with Chase by the way since I'm radical.
I knew I had it in me to write this poem.
I knew I had it in me to change lives.
Change minds. Be an agent of change.
Please clap or at least nominate me for something.
Retweet this on the internet. Use the word *problematic.*
And if poets are the unacknowledged legislators of the world.
And if you actually believe that.

If I didn't think—almost daily—what a coincidence this all is.

What a coincidence that we're here.

Doing this. Being anything.

Just stroking my cock.

Yeah, I'm stroking it hard.

ENVY

Even hotel bartenders
knew we weren't a couple.
Though they gave us one check
and left us alone. Sometimes
they looked at me like a woman
making a mistake. Because I was.
A man making a mistake.
Happy to have you for a drink.
Happy to open a tab when you left
which you always did.
Isn't it terrible there aren't
villains in real life?
It would be so easy to hate you.
I've never been the type of person
to think about planning a wedding.
Walked 8th Street alone in all seasons.
Preferred it. Been simple. Been awful.
I would have been anything with you.
I've punched the bathroom walls
at those bars so many times.
Thought of the women you're fucking.
Jerked off instead of pissing.
Had a bottle before dinner.
At some point it started snowing.
I didn't have the right shoes for the weather.
I don't like scarves. I don't like gloves.
I don't like anything
that prevents me from the interior.
All my life, all I've wanted
is to touch where that is.

GREED

Everything I shouldn't want, I do.
Gin. Leather. Being a bad homosexual.
Complaining about loneliness
and booking a flight to the Maldives.
Complaining about loneliness
and asking everyone to leave me alone.
(What a life I'm having!
What a cruel season this is!)
When I say I'm out of fucks
I mean take out your wallet.
Make more money. Buy a boat.
Put me on that boat and take my photo.
Help me stop feeling. Give me a pill.
Another drink. One more August.
Take out your assets.
Take out your weapon.
Take out your diversified stocks portfolio.
But what I really want to know is:
how do you imagine using me for your interests?
And what I also want to know is:
how American does it feel
every time you are numb.

ALONE IN THE MALDIVES

The blues were endless.
I watched the boats
move across the horizon in bed.
Ate fruit. Wore nothing.
Remembered the first time I saw you.
When neither of us knew what we wanted.
And everything was better without knowledge.
Which is so close to sadness
there has to be gin now.
There have to be pills, palms, peonies.
Rain on the pool. Rain on the sea. Rain on the sailors.
Rain in my mouth where your hands used to be.

BIRTHDAY IN PALM SPRINGS

The winds made me crazy.
At King's Highway diner
I did tarot for the waitress
and she drew a heart on my bill.
Every day I watched a boy
play dead in the pool.
His friends laughed at him
from their beach chairs.
"I won," he'd yell.
"I beat all of you again."

When a stranger in a cowboy hat
asked if I was born in 1984
I didn't answer. I stared
at the San Jacinto Mountains
in his BMW. He said, "pull
the seat back," so I did.
Most nights I played alive
at the bar, after dinner,
the hotel bathrooms, a fire
pit near my room.

"You remind me of no one,"
the cowboy said. It was
supposed to be a compliment.
I was supposed to be older
but I've been six years old
since I got here. Trying to write
this poem since I can remember.
Trying not to die and I don't
want to die here. No one has been good.
No one has known what I am.

NEXT TIME

The traffic eased and the light changed.
Sometimes crossing the park
they imagined more than the park.
Sometimes crossing the park
they imagined nothing and spoke of little.
A friend moved. A friend married.
New plays opened. The bars filled.
And in the middle of most sentences
they thought they would say something different.
And in the middle of some days
they thought they would be someone else.
More films about love. More books about war.
Did anything really surprise them?
They wore black to the party. Drank often.
Asked for things they had quit.
Saw people they knew not to see.
That was half of it anyway.
The rest couldn't be gotten.
The rest ended in restlessness.
Open signs glowed. The nights passed.
The mornings repeated away.

TRIPPING IN THE USA

Got to JFK
and took the 10:40
to Miami.
Felt like Vegas
on a Sunday morning.
Felt like crying
but was too hungover
and too tired.
Landed.
Threw up.
Texted.
Showered.
C brought blow
to The Standard
and we jumped
in the cold plunge.
Took a car
to Over Under
with a bunch of
straight bros
talking crypto.
Crushed adderall
in the bathroom.
Took the vitamin
in my pocket.
Someone's dick.
Someone's dick pic.
Someone's wasted boyfriend.
4 tequilas. 2 vodkas.
Checked my hair
on my phone.
Let my fly

go undone.
Used a crucifix
as a coke spoon
and nothing's really
what it seems.
It's so boring.
To be a person in
these United States of Whatever.
A person in summer.
A person without you.
I'm fine, I said to the driver.
Put my sunglasses on
and we talked about Trump.
Went to Mayfair.
Amal. Nathan's. Twist.
I have so much to tell you
but I passed out with clothes on.
Passed out again. Window open.
Then got up for crunches.
Googled Christian Bale
in *American Psycho*
and went for a beach run.
Had the 22 at Puerto Sagua
where I sat at the counter
and counted the men
and the likes
and your texts
and the tourists.
Pisces moon.
Aries sun.
It was all
just like heaven
but Vegas. Miami.
The trees
on Meridian

lit up like Xmas.
The xanax
inside me.
The poppers.
The torsos.
The past.
Took my mask
off. Felt free.
Felt nothing.
Felt dead in
these United States of Whatever.
Packed for London.
Got to Paris.
Berlin.
San Francisco.
The Maldives.
Yeah kill me
but America's where
I will die
that's the life
that I'm in for.
And if your pills
have stopped working
and if the drugs
are less pure now.
California. The desert.
Shrooms with a Gemini
on my birthday
and the photo booth
at The Ace didn't work.
And my aura was blue
then my aura was purple.
There's no going back
said the guy
on Palm Canyon.

There's no real
enlightenment
and nothing to pray for.
On the 2:55 to JFK
I threw up again
and again and again.
Took the FDR down.
Walked to Houston.
The wind on my face
my own tongue
in my mouth
and I thought of
the first years.
When everyone
in poetry gave me shit
though not much
has changed
but the fucks
I've run out of.
God bless that.
God's nowhere.
GOD'S COMING
reads the sign
above a parking lot
in these United States of Whatever.
I was too good for you baby.
I know what I'm made of.
So I drank like a saint.
and I drank like an addict.
Lost my passport
my keys and my mind
all at Clando.
Could not stop
putting things
in my body.

Could not stop
reading about victims
and how badly
you all wanted to be one.
It was 2016.
And then 2019.
And yeah somewhere
along the way
it felt like the same year.
If you're not performing
how just and moral you are
on the internet
you're the only one winning.
The only one getting laid.
The only one just like Jesus.
Retweet that.
Try dick.
Worship Satan.
What haven't we done
in these United States of Whatever.
Where it's so expensive
to be a real person—
I charged it.
My debt. My loans.
My jeans. My soul
was pure and beautiful
in Bottega Veneta.
God bless America.
What I'm trying to say is
it all sort of passes.
The years we have buried.
The drinks in our glasses.
I wanted to tell you
this all when I saw you
but listen. Nothing

I take is that numbing.
It makes me feel twice
what I'm already feeling.
And most days I'd blow
my brains easy
but exits are boring.
If you forget
who you are
why you're here
where you'll go
what you're doing.
I'm with you.
I'm with you.
I'm with you
forever.

ACKNOWLEDGMENTS

"The Years," "Someone in Paris, France Is Thinking of You," "Monday,"
and "Everything Always" were first published in *The New Yorker*.

"Birthday in Palm Springs" was first published in *Poetry*.

"Today I Love Being Alive" and "Tuesday" were first published in *The Atlantic*.

Thank you to everyone who stuck by me during the years of writing
this book.

Most of all, thank you, God, and God bless America.

Psalm 34:18: "The Lord is close to the brokenhearted and saves those
who are crushed in spirit."

A NOTE ABOUT THE AUTHOR

Alex Dimitrov lives in New York City.

A NOTE ABOUT THE TYPE

This book was set in Arno, a typeface designed by Adobe
principal designer Robert Slimbach in 2007. Its namesake is
the Arno River, which flows through Florence, the city at the
heart of the Italian Renaissance. Inspired by the humanist
letterforms of the fifteenth and sixteenth centuries, Slimbach
designed Arno with the vitality and readability of Venetian and
Aldine book typefaces in mind.

Typeset by North Market Street Graphics
Lancaster, Pennsylvania

Designed by Marisa Nakasone